# The Giar



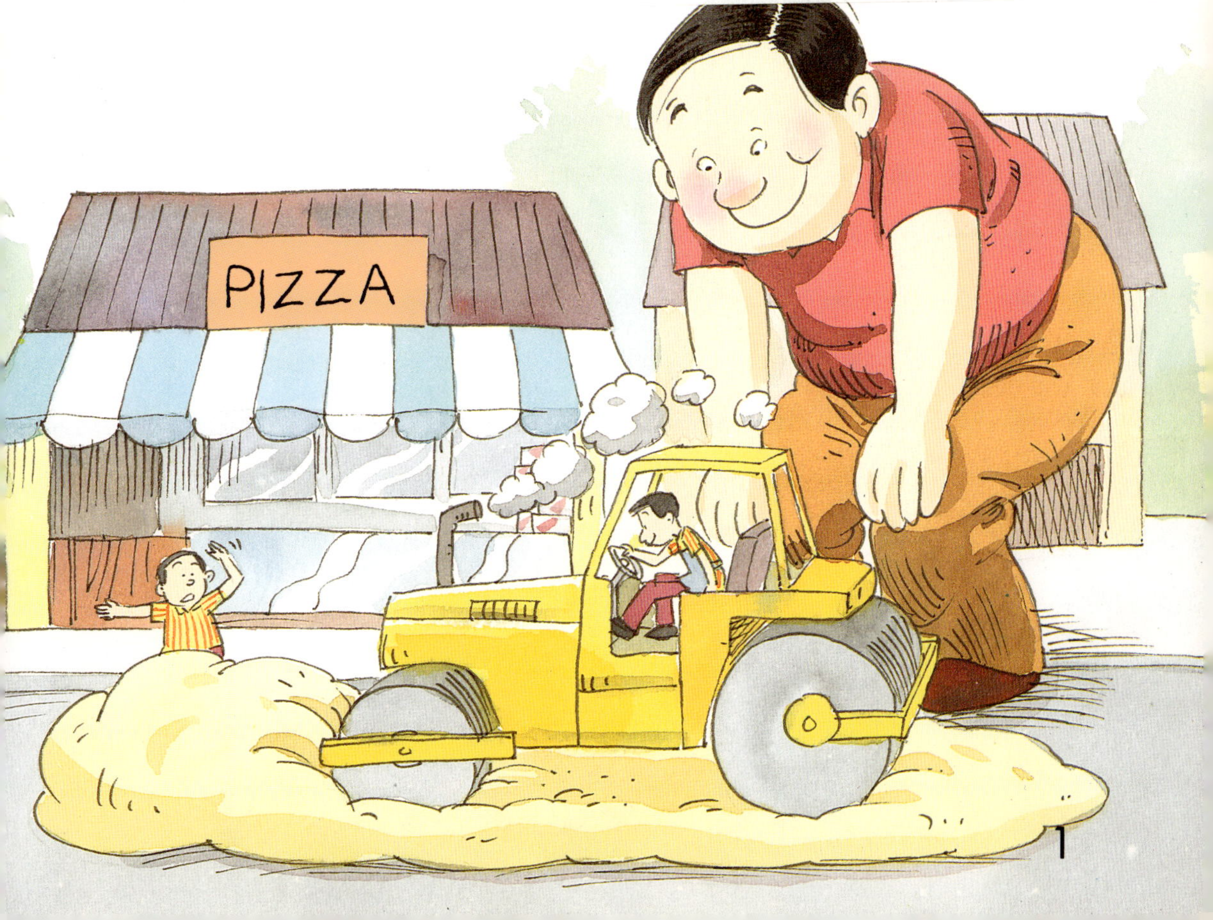

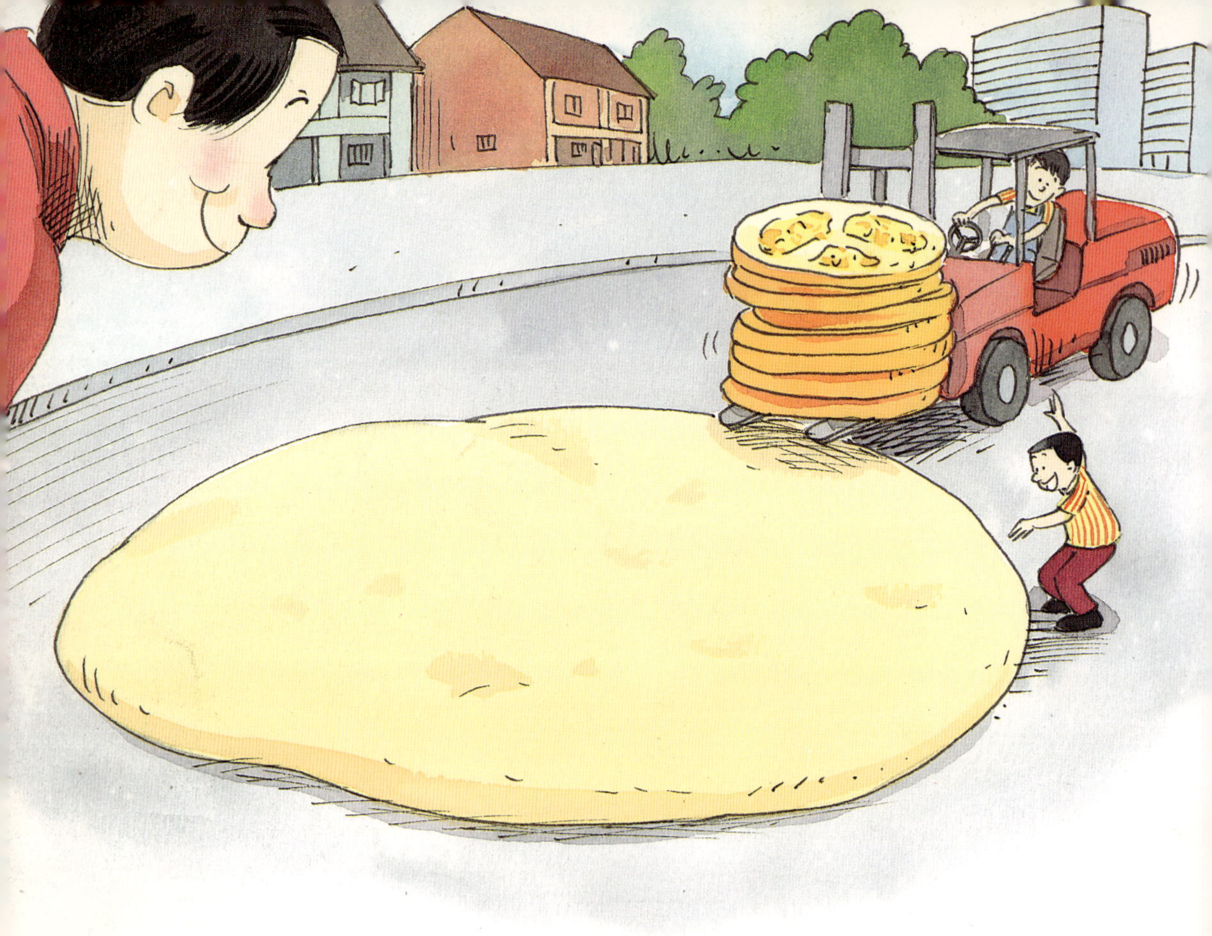

"Put some tomatoes on it."

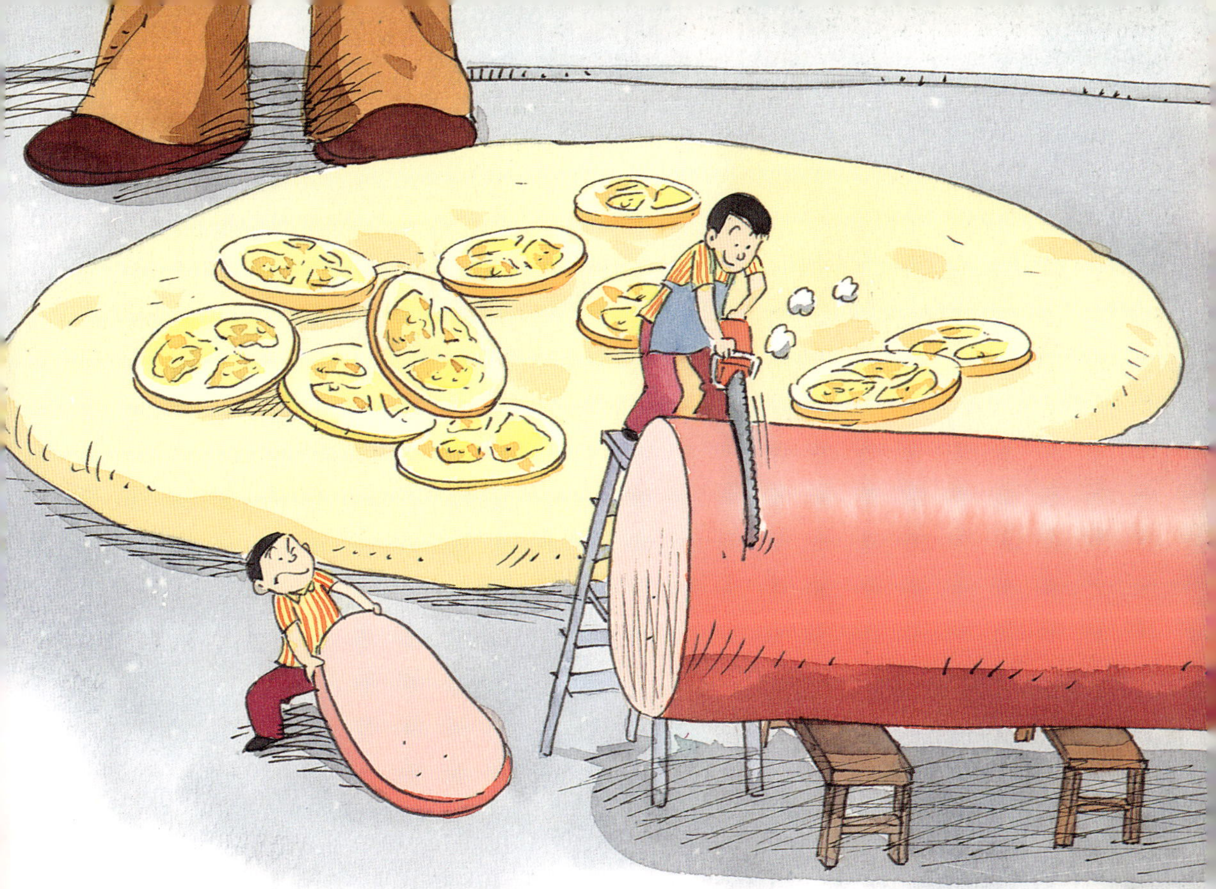

"Put some meat on it."

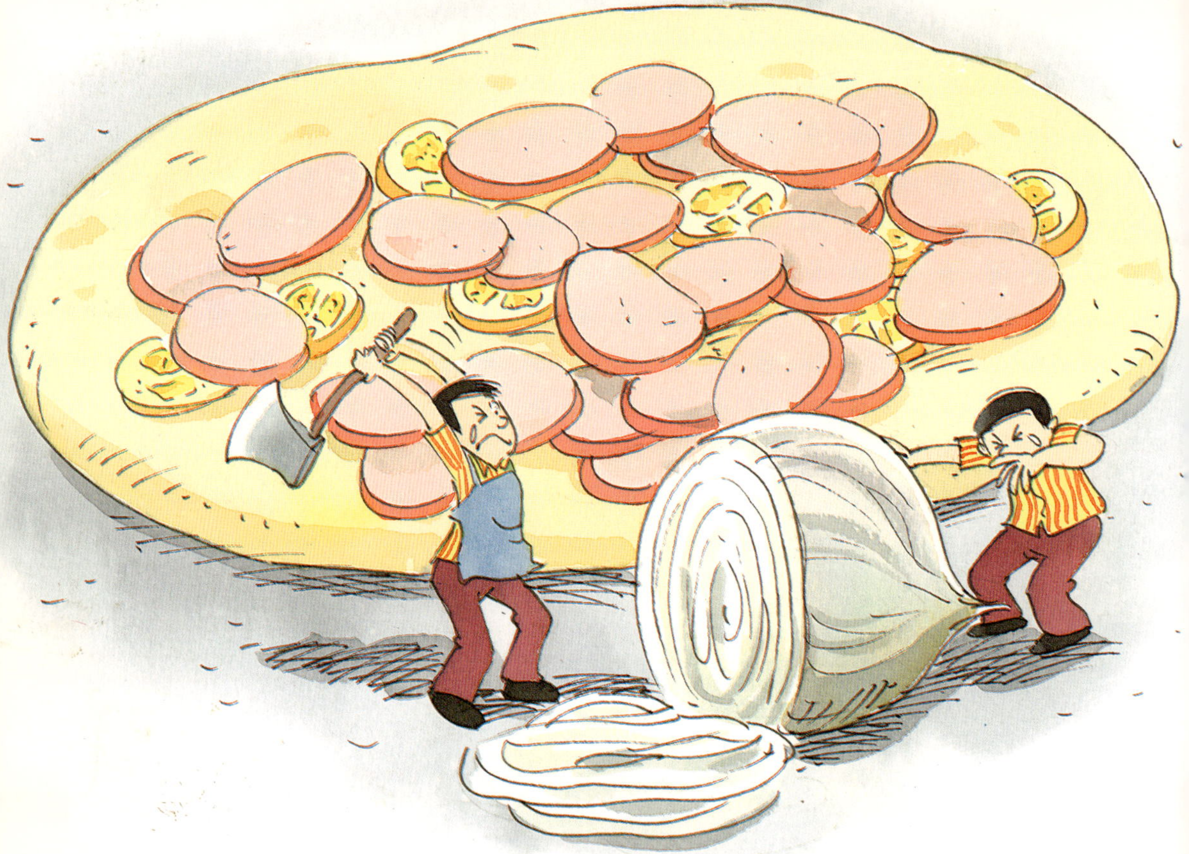

"Put some onions on it."

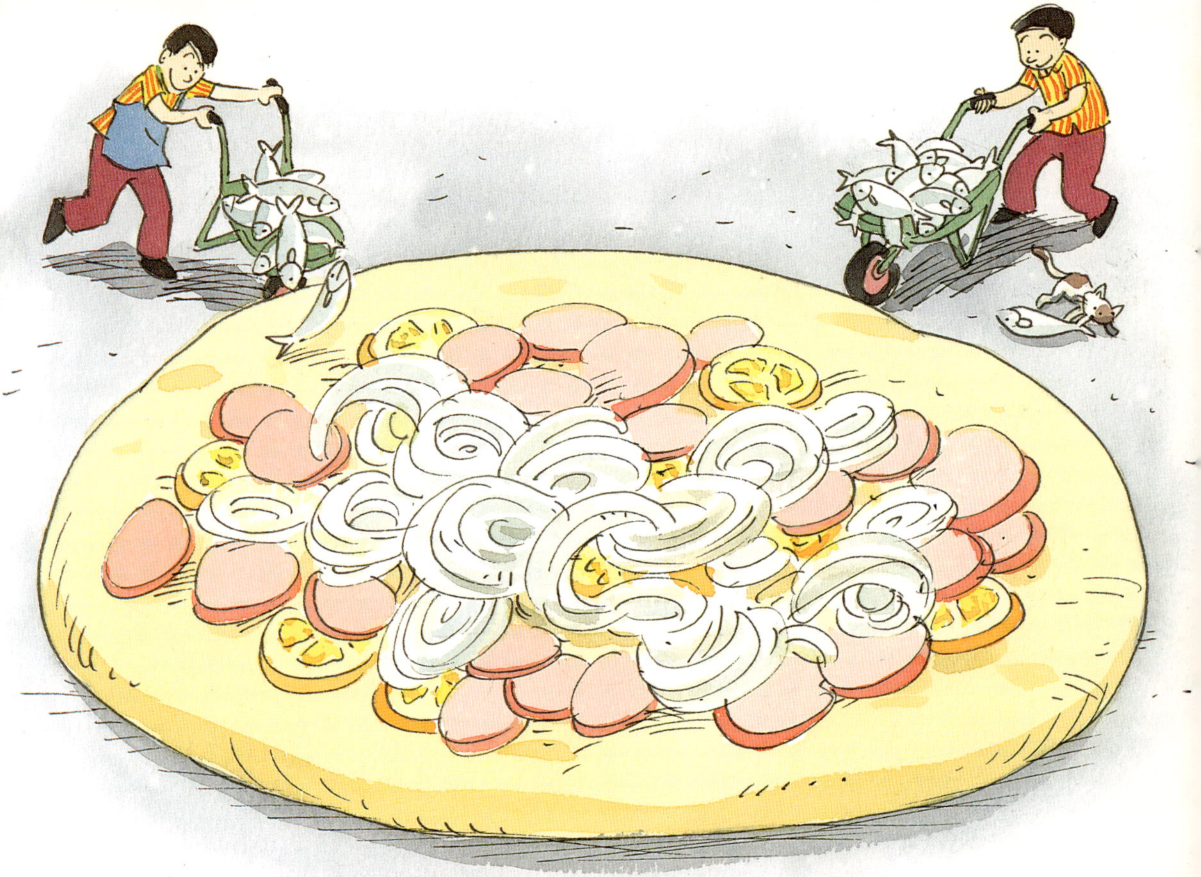

"Put some fish on it."

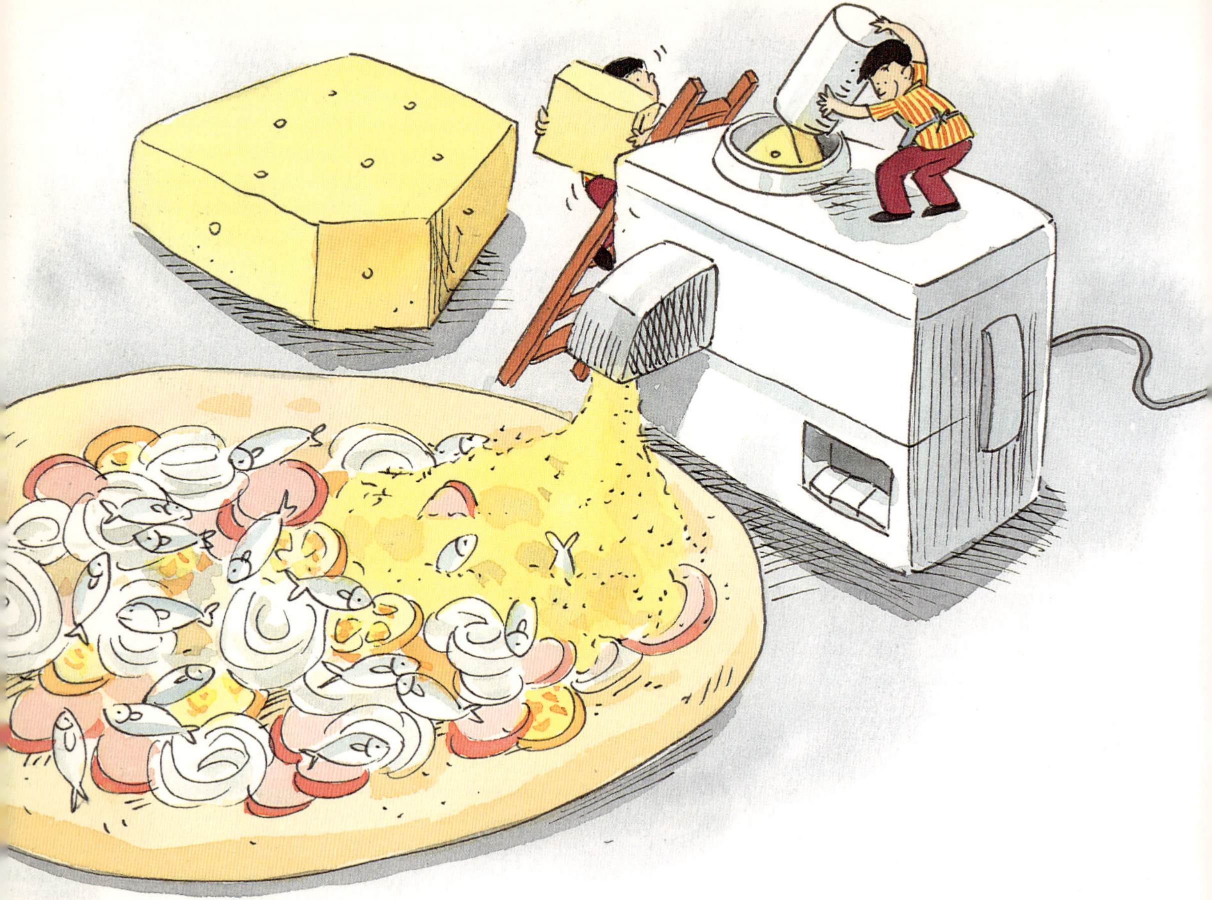

"Put some cheese on it."

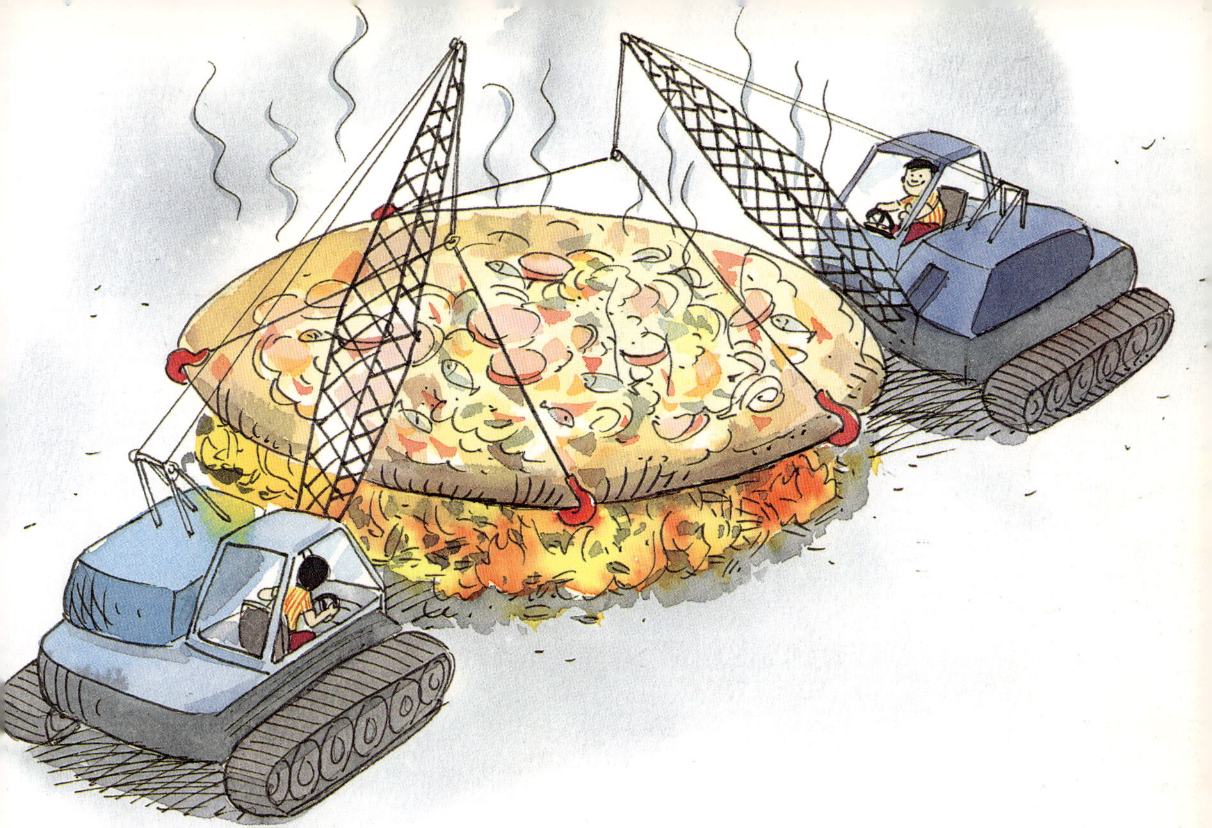

"Cook it!"

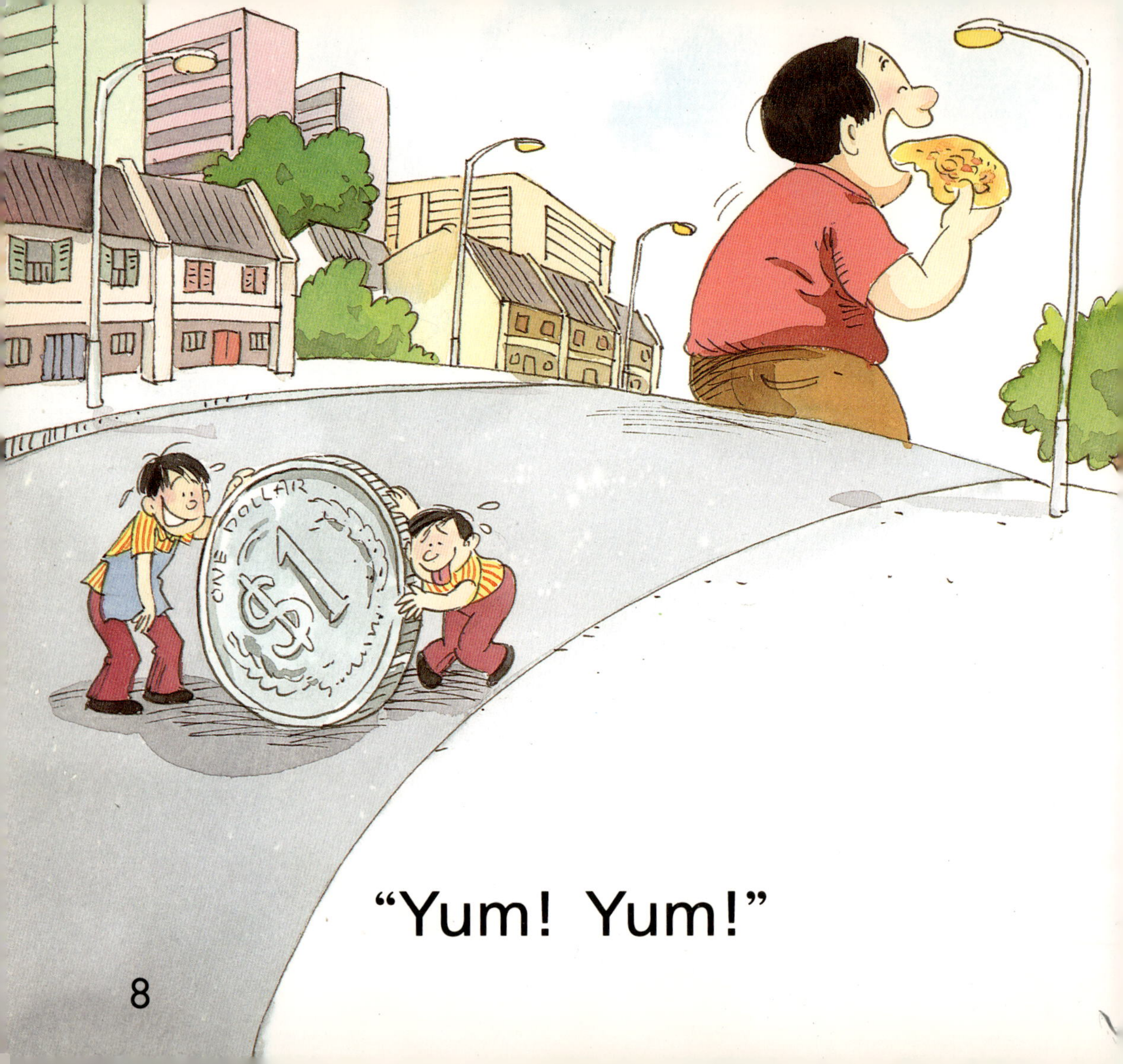


"Yum! Yum!"